Start Your Own Religion

by Timothy Leary

Ronin Publishing, Inc.
Berkeley CA

Published by
Ronin Publishing, Inc.
PO Box 22900
Oakland, CA 94609
www.roninpub.com

Editor:	Beverly A. Potter	docpotter.com
Cover & Interior Design:	Beverly A. Potter	
Cover Design:	Brian Groppe	briangroppe.com
Cover Illustration:	John Thompson	magdalena4@mac.com

<u>Fonts</u>: Venis family, Blockobats (Jeremy Simon), Couchlover, Spunkflakes (Spunk!), TeguilaHill (Celly), Uncle
Stinky, & MisterFrisky by Chank; Abadi MT by The Monotype Corp., Air Force, Babe-alicious, & Fantastic
Creatures by Iconian, CircusDog, Handheld, & MatrixDot by Ethan Dunham of Font Head, Clunky & Mister
Filthy by Nerfect Type & Britton Walters, DoggyPrint by Astigmatic One Eye, Underground by Nick Curis,
Ale and Wenches by Nate Piekos, Harrington by The Font Bureau, Basehead by Terrence Calcium, Bedbug &
Easily amused by Jakob Fischer, Big Cheese by Screen Fonts, Zoomorphica by David D. Nalle of Scriptorium;
MesoDeko, AztecDaySigns & Hypnotica by Deniart Systems; PipelineRusted by ITF, Bloodfest by B. O.
Nelson-BrainEaters Font Co., BakerSignet, & Blackoak by Adobe.

<u>Illustrations</u>: Sacred Aums by The Mathavasis of Kauai's Hindu Monastery (books@hindu.org); Phil Frank of
San Francisoc Chronicle; Hemera Photo Objects; Dover; clipart.com; *Psychedelic Prayers.*

Library of Congress Card Number: 2005921451
Distributed to the book trade by **Publishers Group West**
Printed in the United States by **United Graphics**

Table of Contents

Ronin Books
by Timothy Leary

Table of Contents continued

You are a God.

Live like one!

Timothy Leary, the Crazy Wisdom Guru

Preface

by Wes 'Scoop' Nisker

I love the title of this book, because that's what happened. We made up our own religions. Or else we adapted new ones that came from the other side of the planet, or we patched together our own personal crazy quilt (security blanket) of beliefs, rituals and symbols, gathered from all the world's religious cultures. We knew that the divine was present in all of it. The drugs told us that, loud and clear. Tim also told us that, and we believed him because, after all, he was "the high priest."

So I now have a private altar in my home, filled with "graven" images. I sit before my altar in meditation, and sometimes look to it for inspiration. When I was growing up none of my relatives or any of the Jewish people we knew had an altar in their house. I can hear my grandmother saying, "Altar, schmaltar! So, the synagogue is not good enough for you?"

On my altar is a bronze statue of the dignified, meditating Buddha, a wooden head of the Chinese "laughing Buddha," a picture of the Hindu goddess Kali, a little carved statue of the Native trickster coyote, a Thai potency amulet, and an assortment of nature fetishes. Other images and pictures get shuffled onto my altar from time to time, and I must admit that occasionally I get confused about which deity to call upon for a particular problem I may be having. This confusion would not arise with Jehovah, of course, because He's an all-purpose God.

Looking at my altar, I also recognize that most of the deities represented are illegal immigrants: none of them has a green card to work in America. In fact, many have been smuggled into this country by people like me, citizens of empire who traveled around the colonies, looking for new ways of being and praying.

In the past half century, a religious revolution has taken place in the Western world; a mythological upheaval. This kind of

> The old gods are dead or dying and people everywhere are searching, asking: What is the new mythology to be, the mythology of this unified earth as of one harmonious being?
>
> —Joseph Campbell

thing seems to happen every few millennia. Consider, for instance, that the descendants of a family living near the Mediterranean could have gone from believing in Chronos to believing in Zeus, then Jupiter, Jehovah, and finally adding Jesus, in just the last five thousand years. Even among the gods there is occasional regime change.

Many middle-class Americans born after World War II grew up to reject the religion of their birth. As Ram Dass says, "I'm only Jewish on my parents side." Often we were the first in our families to go to college, where we were taught how to doubt and deconstruct everything our parents, government and churches had ever taught us. Many of us came to regard a belief in a personal god as ridiculous as a belief in Santa Claus.

Could there really be a supreme "being" who witnessed and judged our every action, and who would actually listen to our prayers?

Our doubts were reflected in the popular culture. For instance, for the week of April 8, 1966, *Time* magazine's cover story was entitled, "Is God Dead?" The editors at Time chose not to answer that question, but the very fact that it was raised didn't bode well for the deity. Even if God wasn't dead, it seems He may have been having a mid-life crisis.

Into the spiritual vacuum of America in mid-century came psychedelic drugs and the subculture of the hippies. Just being a hippie was kind of like being in a new religion. We didn't exactly believe in a god, but we celebrated all of them, and the goddesses too, and wore their symbols and chanted their praises. The ideas of Joseph Campbell and Carl Jung were in the air, and we understood that all religious stories were just stories, which meant that we could embrace them all as beautiful creations of human longing and imagination. Besides, as Zen scholar and raconteur Alan Watts put it, "We do not need a new religion or a new bible. We need a new experience—a new feeling of what it means to be 'I.'"

The hippie subculture was the expression of a spiritual revival, a call to love and celebrate existence.

In 1967, the *San Francisco Oracle*, a Haight-Ashbury underground journal promoted the first "Human Be-In," by declaring: "The *spiritual* revolution will be manifest and proven. In unity we will shower the country with waves of ecstacy and purification." A flyer handed out at the 1967 anti-war march on the Pentagon began: "We Freemen, of all colors of the spectrum, in the name of God, Ra, Anubis, Osiris, Tlaloc, Quetzalcoatl, Thoth, Chukwu..." and on and on, listing the names of gods from almost every culture on the planet.

The hippies were mythological collage artists. We bowed down to it all, trying to feel our connection to the universe, our bodies, the natural world, the movement of the planets (What's your sign?), the mystery itself. Since we couldn't seem to find the connection through our churches and synagogues we started looking for it on the

fringes of society and in other spiritual traditions. We turned to ancient practices such as meditation, breathwork, sweat lodges, tarot, astrology, music and drugs.

A primary source of the new religious expressions that arose in the past half century was LSD and other psychedelic drugs. They gave people at least the temporary ability to see through the fictions of ego and separation that seem to engulf humanity. As people experimented with psychedelics they also realized that the Taoists, Hindus and Buddhists, as well as many indigenous and esoteric spiritual traditions were already well versed in the feelings of oceanic oneness and compassion. Both Tim Leary and Richard Alpert (Ram Dass) found that their visionary drug experiences were best explained by Asian spiritual texts, and they advised people to use the *Tibetan Book of the Dead* and the *Tao Te Ching* for guidance during LSD sessions. People began to understand that what they were experiencing on psychedelics was not just hallucinatory play, but a traditional mystical perception of reality.

For me, as for many others, the teachings of the Buddha spoke directly to my newly expanding consciousness, as well as to my confusion. Buddhist meditation practices promised to take me

beyond my seemingly perpetual identity crisis, and also offered me the solace of vast perspectives on our turbulent historical era. As Nietzsche wrote, "Buddhism is a religion for the end and fatigue of civilizations."

Out of our confusion and searching, recent generations have started a spiritual revival in the West, loosely known as new age. Closely allied, and growing ever more so, is the modern environmental movement, with its quasi-spiritual, neo-pagan overtones. Perhaps some new paradigm is being born that will take us safely into the future. For now, however, we are experiencing a backlash to our divine tinkering, reflected in religious fundamentalism and *holy* wars all over the world. Fear of modernity, relativism and secular science has turned many people back to the old time religions as they try to find some certainty, a refuge from this time of turmoil.

I may have a solution to humanity's current religious troubles. First, let me be clear that I don't think it is wrong or stupid to believe in a god. In fact, I love the gods and goddesses, every single one of them. (If you love them all, then you're covered for sure.) The only real problem with the gods are the humans who believe in them. Of course you might ask, who's fault are they?

Displaying a combination of ignorance and arrogance, people keep killing each other in the name of some particular god, or warring over the holy places where a god supposedly walked around or spoke to some prophets. These so-called *holy* wars have taken place throughout human history, but you would think that by now we would know better. Indeed, the relativity of the gods was noticed way back in the fifth century B.C. by the historian Xenophanes, who wrote, "The Ethiopians say that their gods are snub-nosed and black, the Thracians that theirs have light blue eyes and red hair."

A lot of people still say they know for sure who god is, and if you don't believe in their particular god they will kill you. Others say that if you don't believe in their god, they promise that

> God has no religion.
>
> —Mahatma Gandhi

when you die their god will put you in a burning hot cave where nasty, horned creatures will stick pitch-forks into you and make you scream in pain, forever and ever. Apparently some gods will do that to you if you don't believe in them!?

But why should we care if people call god by a different name than we do? Can you imagine any self-respecting god saying, with menace, "Hey buddy, what did you call me?" Why should you be bothered if someone calls god "Omega," "Felix," or "Martha Reeves and the Vandellas?" In fact, I can imagine that someday the heavens will part, and we will all hear a booming voice saying, "Humans! You *all* got my name wrong!" (Pause) "And I forgive you."

Why should god even have a name? I would say there's a fair chance that god isn't even a *being*, or at least not some human-like being. Do you think we are so good looking that a god—who could look like anything or nothing—would actually want to look like us, with nose hairs or butt-cheeks? "Vanity of van-ity," sayeth the Preacher. "All is vanity."

Even if you aren't a believer, I would guess that most of you reading this will have a certain image of god—and he's an Italian! He's got a long flowing white beard and long hair, and looks somewhat like an aging bohemian. *Cool, man!* I'm referring, of course, to the god who lives up there on the ceiling of the Sistine Chapel. The Italians were the ones who gave us the image of god as that buffed, charismatic creator with the life-giving finger.

If you'll remember, the Jews said we were not supposed to make a graven image of "Him" because "He" was much too great, and no one could ever gaze on "His" face. (At least we knew that this god was male.) But when the Jewish god came down to meet with people He always hid inside a bush, or only let himself be heard as a disembodied voice. That was before the Italians inherited the Jewish god and couldn't resist trying to paint Him.

By the way, the Jews really had a genius idea with this god who you couldn't see; a god that has no form. For one thing, it saves a lot of money on statues. You don't have to put a golden calf on your altar, which could fall off and break.

Anyway, here's my suggestion for how to deal with all our god problems, once and for all. First we call all the gods together for a "summit meeting." Maybe this meeting could be held on Mt. Olympus, or somewhere in the Himalayas, where there are already a lot of gods around who could host the gathering. (There will have to be separate tables: Bacchus needs wine, whereas Buddha won't touch the stuff; Demeter wants corn for dinner, Jehovah likes lamb; Zoroaster wants candles for a center-piece, while Tor would like an ice sculpture.)

Once we got all the gods together, we would beseech them—all of us beseeching our own particular deity—to do humanity a great big favor and decide on a common name. Since I'm the only one working on this project, I will take the liberty to propose this new name.

First of all, if you'll notice, many of the names we already use for deities end in the syllable "ah." Jehov*ah;* All*ah;* Brahm*a;* Tar*a;* Diana; Krishn*a.* So maybe we could get the gods to accept the common nick-name "Ah." (I haven't been hit by lightning yet, so maybe I'm onto something here.)

Ah is the first sound that most of us make when we are born, "w...aaaah!" and the last sound we make as we die, crying or sighing, "Ah...." So both the first and last moments of our life would automatically become a prayer. I suppose people could still use their special tribal names for god, but emphasize the last vowel "ah" and we would all agree that we are talking about the same ultimate, almighty. Totally ah-some!

Another possibility is to give our highest deity the name "Ma," which is the same word in almost all human languages, referring to mother. Then, instead of looking up toward "our father who art in heaven" as we pray, we would look down at the earth, the womb of all life, the goddess who the Greeks called "Gaia." (There's another "ah," for you.)

Maybe we could even use both names, Ah *and* Ma. We would divide god into two, a male and female, yin and yang, just as it was for many humans in our ancient history. "Ah Ma! Ma Ah! Ah-ha Ma!" The possibilities for songs and praises are endless. For instance, everybody open your mouth wide and say "Ah!" (God "the doctor" is in the house.)

If we put our hearts and minds into it, we will soon have another new religion here.

—Wes "Scoop" Nisker

Wes "Scoop" Nisker is an author, radio commentator, Buddhist meditation teacher, and performer. His bestselling books include *Essential Crazy Wisdom, The Big Bang, The Buddha, and the Baby Boom,* and *Buddha's Nature.* Mr. Nisker has studied Buddhist meditation for three decades with teachers in Asia and America, and for the past 15 years has been leading his own retreats and workshops in Buddhist insight meditation and philosophy at venues internationally. He is an affiliate teacher at the Spirit Rock Meditation Center in Woodacre, California, and the founder and co-editor of the international Buddhist journal "Inquiring Mind." For his appearance schedule and to acquire CD's of his radio and performance work go to www.wnisker.com.

Crazy Wisdom Guru

1

Introduction

Check out the history books and read about the years 987 to 1000. In those days a lot of fruit loops were running around stirring up trouble. A thousand years ago Grand Prince Vladimir of Russia started a religious Cold War by joining the Eastern Orthodox Catholic Church. The Persians and Arabs and Christians were waging a Holy War. People were scared and confused back then—just as they are today

We are seeing similar irrational kookiness, messianic megalomanias, mass insanities, apocalyptic paranoias, end-of-world prophecies; demented demagogues, Holy Wars, crazy crusades, lunatic leaders, disharmonic divergences, and thousands of just plain old four-square evangelical bad trips. They're just warm-ups for the eccentricities and terror-activated manias to come.

Most of the violence and angry politics that are apparent these days pit one biblical God against another. It's the Roaring 9th Century all over again! Feudal Super Bowl crusader time! My God versus your Great Satan! Israel versus Rome versus Byzantium. Shi'ites versus Sunnis. Hindus versus Buddhists. Hindus versus Sikhs. Bosnia, Croatia, Serbia. Jehovah versus Allah for the world championship. The Taliban versus The Great Society.

It's your standard right-wing, strident, millenarian kook show.

Predestination, here we come. An appeal to the

chosen people. An expectation of the imminent and miraculous intervention of God or his messianic prophet. A belief in the total transformation to the perfect kingdom. An eternal struggle against the Evil Empire.

Fiercely ascetic white-bread puritanism. Anti-abortion, antigay witch-hunting. Pro-school prayer, pro-creationist "science," What most astonishes and disturbs, however, is the shamanic power of evangelical television show preachers. The services are designed to produce an altered state of consciousness, a classic voodoo hypnotic trance.

Hey, the guy's possessed!

The show productions are that of state-of-the art prime-time television, using the same slick, commercial techniques that seduce us into buying Coors beer and Extra-Strength Tylenol. The actors who appear on the show look like local news anchors. Dignified while men with white trimmed mustaches that look like a Supreme Court justices. Lovely assistants who look like a models for some sensible home product such as Drano or Roach Motel.

The programs build efficiently toward their climax, namely the invocation of the Deity. Buckle your seat belts, trippers, while the Shaman leans over, his eyes clenched in painful concentration.

When the audience is whipped into a classic trance state and is neurologically vulnerable, the preacher starts to imprint the commercials.

He dials up the sponsor and starts to discuss God's agenda—namely His impatience with what's happening on the planet. Both the preacher and the Almighty Lord are "sick and tired" of God's country being taken over

"Jesus! Jesus!"

by sinners, homosexuals, Democrats, secular humanists, atheistic scientists, communist dupes, pornographers, and, above all, the anti-Christ Iraqians and Iranians.

Meanwhile, the older pious-looking chap next to the preacher—the guy wearing the Episcopal clerical collar—is softly singing, beseeching, "Jesus! Jesus!" It's a gentle, soothing, imploring chorus behind the preacher/shaman.

Eventually the preacher begs the Lord to strengthen and arm his people to deal with his enemies. The "Jesus! Jesus!" chorus increases in volume and tempo. Soon the two of them have worked up a voodoo rhythm. The cameras zoom in for close-ups of the audience, their faces twisted with awe and righteous self-pity. Soon the folks are holding hands, softly chanting and sighing the name of Jesus.

Hey, I've participated in as many trance experiences as anyone. I've tripped out to voodoo rites in Haiti. I've been mesmerized by Gnaoua drummers in Tangier. I've attended Navaho peyote ceremonies, Ken Kesey's acid tests, ganja funeral rituals along the Ganges, sacred mushroom chants in Oaxaca, Pan rites in the Rif mountains of Morocco. I've seen folks holding hands, softly chanting and sighing the name of Jerry Garcia. I've even participated in sunrise davening prayers with Hassidic rabbis.

So swear me in, bailiff, and I'll testify as an expert witness that the born-again rituals of our home-grown southern Pentecostals are authentic head trips, and that TV preachers are performing the classic shamanic role of brainwashing.

"And the Lord was sorry that He had made man on the Earth, and it grieved Him to His heart," reads Genesis: 6. *"So the Lord said, 'I will blot out man whom I have created from the face of the ground, man and beast and creeping things and birds of the air, for I am sorry that I have made them'."*

2

Monotheism

When the power of the shamanic tripping is hooked to a confrontational, monotheistic religious dogma, you've got the potential for major mind games.

The TV preachers tap into the old "One God," Middle Eastern Nurnero Uno, who is congenitally jealous, possessive, and given to vengeful genocide if and when His monopoly is challenged.

As I watch TV preacher/shaman incite hatred of nonbelievers, I am reminded of those familiar television news scenes in which mobs in the streets of Tehran lash themselves with chains into frenzies of sorrowful rage against the Great Satan. Discounting superficial cultural differences, there

Beware of

Great Satan

do seem to be striking similarities between the TV preachers and the Ayatollah. They're both media shamans—electronic wizards who are able to use television to convey magnetizing charisma. And they both head highly efficient political organizations.

Come to think of it, TV preachers and the Ayatollah are mirror images of each other.

Their beliefs stem from the same monotheism. And when they look at each other, guess what they see: **The Great Satan**

.

The lexical meaning of Islam is submission, and adherence to the commands of Allah without objection. This is the true essence of Islam. By obeying Allah and observing His commands, the Muslim would be in harmony with the universe in which he lives, for everything in this universe abides by the commands of Allah.

ENTER THE BABY-BOOMERS

The American obsession with the Cold War came to a screeching halt in the mid-1960s, when the first waves of the babyboom generation—76 million strong—started to hit college. The Dr. Spock people are the first post-Cold War generation. Winston Churchill and Omar Bradley are as alien to them as Ulysses Grant and General Jack Pershing.

The group initiations of the Spock kids occurred not at Anzio Beach or Normandy but at Malibu Beach and Fort Lauderdale. They were the first postnuclear, the first postindustrial, the first electronic generation.

Boomers are extremely individualistic, supremely self-confident, indulged, and ennobled by demand feeding.

These affluent children of a doting adult culture are obsessed with such practical, down-to-earth matters as enriched sex, physical comfort, aesthetic style, and personal growth. Above all, they were and still are consistently antiwar and antidraft.

Mainstream America is now learning what psychedelic researchers learned in the 1960s and what most babyboomers learned in the 1970s: Religious, mystical, visionary possession states are powerful and wonderful—they open the doors of perception, polish our sensory

The real issue here is the separation of state and religious visions.

lenses, shake up the autonomic nervous system, and get the hormones surging—but they're intimate and precious. They shouldn't be imposed on others. And above all, they should be kept out of politics.

Our survival could depend upon staying calm and cooling out the crazies among us.

3

Who Owns The Jesus Property?

I've tried to make sense out of the flap a few years back about the film version of *The Last Temptation of Christ.* Why do fundamentalist Protestants attack this movie inspired by a novel penned by a tormented Greek Catholic, adapted by a guilt-ridden Protestant, and directed by a moody Italian Catholic?

More recently we see the controversary over the runaway bestselling novel, *The DiVinci Code.* Since they all claim to be sincere Christians, why all the rhubarb?

Here's My Theory:

What we have here is a typical bunch of quarreling Christian sects-exactly the same noisy cast of characters who have been profiting from similar theological battles for two millennia. They've bickered, century after century about the trinity or the virgin birth or that always explosive topic, the personality, habits, and human/divine endowments of Jesus.

The sides in these well-publicized debates are usually drawn along geographic lines.

People from North Europe tend to define Jesus and the women in his life as less emotional than people from the Mediterranean do.

the nordics want a jesus like them~ selves, cold and repressed.

The Southerners want a passionate, volatile Jesus— like themselves.

There is a fascinating parallel here with Islam. The angry born-again fundamentalists in Iran and Iraq; the moderate Sunni and Saudi Arabs who are just trying to make a buck on the Mecca tourist trade and the oil wells, but who are forced to band together to resist the highly impractical militants.

ISLAM

This relativistic speculation cheered me up. It showed me, once again, how far our American Christians (and American Jews and Moslems) have evolved from their pesky counterparts in the Olde World. In the Middle East these theological differences are still being fought out with tanks and bombers and poison gas; in Northern Ireland, the dour Protestants and passionate Catholics have at each other with guns and gelignite.

JUST LIKE THE MIDDLE AGES, EXCEPT FOR IMPROVED WEAPONRY.

But here in the U.S. our sectarian Christians merely quarrel like talent agencies disputing who owns the screen rights to the Jesus Christ story.

We're hassling over the ownership to one of the most valuable properties of all time.

Look at the script:

The birth in the manger. The walking on water. The loaves and fishes. The scourging of the money lenders from the Temple. (Well, on second thought, let's not stress that scene.) The betrayal by Judas. The crown of thorns. The ever-popular Crucifixion Climax. The surprise ending Resurrection.

It beats Indiana Jones, doesn't it!

Fundamentalists and television evangelists understandably insist that they have a monopoly on the Jesus Property.

There's no shred of evidence to support this in any court!

There's not a single paper anywhere that says the Christ family, Jesus, Mary, Joseph, etc., signed away these valuable docudrama rights to North European Prot-estants and their descendants in the right wing of the Republican party.

Hey, these Johnny-come-lately Protestants didn't appear on the scene until fourteen centuries after the death scene went down.

to be absolutely frank, the ancestors of these bad-tempered european bible thumpers were running around bare-assed in bear-skins, sacrific-ing virgins to thor the thunder god, when the original christ script was

The televangelists are obviously worried that their alleged monopoly on the $50 billion a year Christ Market will be threatened by passionate Latin and Greek versions that attribute Mediterranean humanity to Christ in contrast to the pale, blonde, plastic doll, blue-eyed killer version that they are peddling. The primordial Greek-Latin image of J. C. is too 'human" and emotional for dogmatic Jerry Falwell or shy, onanistic Jimmy Swaggart, or sexually naieve Jim "Motel" Bakker.

> The primordial Greek-Latin image of J. C. is too 'human" and emotional.

In my scenario of these events,

Jesus and Mary Magdalene and Peter the Fisherman and the rest of the rowdy gang would be laughing their haloes off at this grubby wrangling for the screen rights to their story. After all, the Jewish Jesus, or Yeshuah—the prototype, even older than Greek-Latin versions—seems to have been an easy-going Reform rabbi with a sly sense of humour, a genial, Hin-Jew rabbi like Ram Dass.

Anyway, if the Writers Guild takes an interest, they should demand residuals for Matthew, Mark, Luke, and John, those four hard- working, ink-stained wretches who penned this eternally interesting and controversial script.

4

Born Again Paganism

During their teens the boomers went on an adolescent spiritual binge unequalled since the Children's Crusade.

In their revolt against the factory culture, they reinvented and updated their tribal-pagan roots and experimented with Hinduism, Buddhism, American Indianism, Magic, Witchcraft, Ann Arbor Voodoo, Esalen Yoga, I Ching, Taoism, Exorcism of the Pentagon, 3-D Re-Incarnations, Love-Ins, and Psychedelic Celebrations.

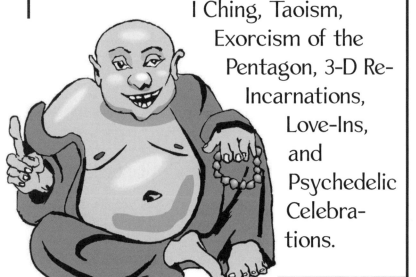

Pan-Dionysus on audiovisual cassettes. Mick Jagger had them sympathizing with the devil. The Beatles had them floating upstream on the Ganges. Jimi Hendrix taught them how to be a voodoo child.

Is there one pre-Christian or third-world metaphor for divinity that some rock group has not yet celebrated on an album cover?

The baby-boomers in their evolving life cycle seem to have reca-pitulated the theological history of our species. Just as monotheism emerged to unify pagan tribes into nations, so did some boomers rediscover fundamentalist, born-again Judaism and Christianity in their young adulthood. Even far-away Islam attracted gourmet blacks and ex-hippies like Cat Stevens. Bob Dylan nicely exemplifies the consumer approach to religion. For twenty five years Dylan browsed thro the spiritual boutiques, dabbin on a dash of Baptist "born aga nibbling at Hassidism, before returning to his old-time faith of sardonic reformed human-ism.

5

Do-It-Yourself-Religion

We can laugh at this trendy shopping around for the custom-tailored, designer God,

But . . .

Behind the faddism
we find a powerful clue.

Recall how Dylan, for example,
preserved his options
and tried to
avoid shoddy
or off-the-rack
soulware.

no "plastic christs that glow in the dark" for bob!

Evolutionism

The real religion here is Evolutionism, based on the classic humanist, transcendental assumptions:

- God is not a tribal father, nor a feudal lord, nor an engineer-manager of the universe.

- There is no God—in the singular—except you at the moment.

- There are as many Gods—in the plural—as can be imagined. Call them whatever you want. They are free agents like you and me.

- You can change and mutate and keep improving.

Buddha, Krishna, Gurdjieff, taught:

The aim of your life is to
take care of yourself so
you can take care of others.

The idea is
to keep
"trading up"
to a "better"
philosophy-
theology.

This generation, we recall, was disillusioned by the religions, politics, and economics of their parents. Growing up with the threat of nuclear war, the assassination of beloved leaders, a collapsing industrial system, an impossible national debt, religious fundamentalisms—Christian-Jewish-Islamic—that fanatically scream hatred and intolerance, acquired immune deficiencies, and uncomprehending neglect of the ecology, they have developed a healthy skepticism about collective solutions.

Individual Navigation

No wonder the baby-boom generation has created a psychology of individual navigation.

The basic idea is self-responsibility. You just can't depend on anyone else to solve your problems. You gotta do it all by yourself... with a little help from your friends.

Singularity.

Since God #1 appears to
be held hostage back
there by the blood-thirsty
Persian ayatollah, by the
telegenic Polish pope,
and the Moral Majority . . . .

. . . . there's only one logical alternative.

Steer your own course!

you and your dear friends must start your own religion.*

 The Temple, of course, is your body.

 Your minds write the theology.

 And the holy spirit emanates from that infinitely mysterious intersection between your brain and the brains of your team.

*The attainment of even the suburbs of paradise involves good navigation and planning on your part.

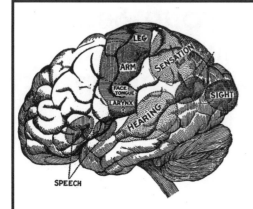

Your Brain Is God!

Hell is a series of redeemable errors.

A detour caused by failure to check the trip maps.

A losing streak.

Reward yourself

for making choices that lead
to friendship and pleasure.

Build a cybernetic cycle of positive feedback

Only from a state of free selfhood can
any truly compassionate signals be sent
to others

6

Create
A Personal State

The management and piloting of a singularity leads to

a very busy career.

Become

a free agent.

As an individual, establish yourself as

a religion,

a country,

a corporation,

an information network,

and a neurologia universe.

Of course, it is necessary to maintain personal equivalents of all the departments and operations of the bureaucracies that perform these duties.

A free agent:

☆ Formulates private alliances,

☆ Formulates personal political platforms,

☆ Conducts one's own domestic and foreign relations,

☆ Establishes trade policies, defense and security programs.

On the up side, one is free from dependence on bureaucracies, an inestimable boon. Free agents can, of course, make temporary deals with organizations and officials thereof.

If countries have histories and mythic origins, why shouldn't you?

7

Develop A Personal Mythology

Search and research your very own genetic memory banks, the Old Testaments of your DNA-RNA, including past incarnations, Jungian archetypes and funky pre-incarnations in any future

you can imagine.

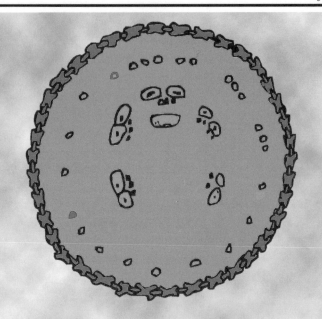

You and your friends can do anything that the great religions and empires and racial groups have done in the name of their God.

There's no way your Personal State could produce the persecutions and massacres and bigotries of the past and present.

There's only one of you, and even with
the help of your friends the amount of
damage individuals
can do is insignificant
compared with
that collective.

aND YOU'RE
CERtaIN tO δO
It BEttER
BECaUSE ...
WELL, LOOK at
thEIR tRaCK
RECORδS.

You can choose
your Gods
to be smart,
compassionate,
cute and
goofy.

8

Religious Discovery

That intermediate manifestation of the divine process which we call the DNA code has spent the last 2 billion years making this planet

a Garden of Eden.

An intricate web has been woven, a delicate fabric of chemical-electrical-seed-tissue-organism-species.

A dancing, joyous harmony of energy

transactions is rooted in the 12 inches of topsoil

which covers the

rock

METAL

fire

core of this planet.

Into this

Garden of Eden

each human being
is born perfect.

We were all born divine mutants, the DNA code's best answer to joyful survival on this planet. An exquisite package for adaptation based on 2 billion years of consumer research (RNA) and product design (DNA).

Each baby,

although born perfect,

immediately finds himself in a

imperfect,

artificial,

disharmonious

social system that systematically
robs him of his divinity.

Individual societies begin in harmonious adaptation to the environment and, like individuals, quickly get trapped into nonadaptive, artificial, repetitive sequences.

And the social systems? Where did they come from?

When the individual's behavior and con-sciousness get hooked to a routine sequence of external actions,

he is a dead robot, and . . .

When the individual's behavior and con-sciousness get hooked to a routine sequence of external actions, he is a dead robot, and

it is time for him to die and . . . be reborn.

It is time to

ᗞRop out,

turn on,

tune in!

This period of robotization. It is called the **Kali Yuga**, the **Age of Strife and Empire**, the peak of so called "civilization".

This relentless law of death, life. Change is the rhythm of the galaxies and the seasons, the rhythm of the seed.

It never stops.

9

Drop Out, Turn On, Tune In

If you've become a dead robot with your consciousness hooked into routines,

and **more** routines. . . .

Drop Out

Detach yourself from the
external social drama which
is as dehydrated and ersatz
as TV.

Turn On

Find a sacrament which returns you to the temple of God—your own body.

Go out of

your mind.

Get High.

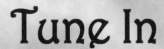

Tune In

Drop back in to express it.
Start a new sequence of
behavior that

reflects your

vision.

Be Reborn

Become your

highest vision of

you.

Death. Life. Structure.

The sequence must continue.

You cannot stand still.

D. L. S.

D. L. S. D. L. S. D.

L. S. D. L. S. D. L.

S. D. L. S. D. . .

American Reality

Any action that is not a conscious expression of the drop-out-turn-on-tune-in-drop-out rhythm is the dead posturing of robot actors on the fake-prop TV studio stage set that is called American reality.

The *wise person* devotes his life exclusively to the religious search—for therein is found the only ecstasy, the only meaning.

Actions which are conscious expressions of the turn-on, tune-in, drop-out rhythm are *religious*.

Anything else is a
competitive quarrel
over television studio props
or a Hollywood love sharing.

10

How
To Turn On

To turn on is to detach from the rigid addictive focus on the fake-prop TV studio set and to refocus on the natural energies within

 YOUR BODY.

TO TURN ON:

You go out of your mind and. . .

1. Come to your senses—focus on sensory energies.

2. Resurrect your body—focus on somatic energies.

3. Drift down cellular memory tracks beyond the body's space-time—focus on cellular energies.

4. Decode the genetic code.

<u>Note well</u>: At each of these levels—sensory, somatic, cellular, molecular—attention can be directed at energy changes within or without the body. If attention is directed externally during the session, the outside world is experienced in terms of a nonsymbolic energy-language focus.

Be careful.

This can be shocking.

When you've T U R N E D O N, the props of the TV studio stage set are suddenly experienced:

1. **As sensory**—the room is alive, out of control, exploding with light and sound;

2. **As somatic**—the room is alive undulating with digestive rhythm;

3. **As cellular**—all props and actors take on a stylized, mythic, reincarnate hue;

4. **As molecular**—all props and actors shimmer impersonally as vibratory mosaics.

stage set recognition
eliminates fear and
confusion.

11
Learn to Pray

To turn on,

you must learn how **to pray.**

you need maps and manuals to turn on,.

Prayer is the compass,
the gyroscope for
centering and
stillness.

You can not
pray to an
external power.
That is begging

Prayer is ecstatic
communication with your
inner navigational
computer.

There are those transition moments of terror, isolation, reverence, gratitude... when there comes that need to communicate with the energy source you sense in yourself and around you—at the highest and best level you are capable of. There is a need for a straight, pure, non-game language. **This is prayer.** This need has been known and sensed for thousands of years.

All prayers are communications with higher, freer energies.

When the ecstatic cry is called
for, you must be ready to address
Higher Intelligence. **You must be
ready to pray.** When you have lost
the need to address the Higher
Intelligence, you are a dead man
in a world of dead symbols.

Conventional prayers, for the
most part, have degenerated
into parrot rituals, slogans,
mimicked verbalizations,
appeals for game help.

You are a God.

Pray like one!

12

Psychedelic
Prayers

Manifestation of the Mystery

Gazing, we do not see it.

We call it empty space.

Listening, we do not hear it.

We call it silence.

Reaching, we do not grasp it.

We call it intangible.

But here . . . we spin through
it.

Electric, silent, subtle.

Take In–Let Go

To breathe in
You must first breathe out.
Let go.

To hold
You must first open your hand.
Let go.

To be warm
You must first be naked.
Let go.

The Unity of Nothing

The **nothing** at the center
  of the thirty-spoke wheel...
The **nothing** of the clay vase ...
The **nothing** within the four walls ...

The goal of the game is to
  go beyond the game.

You **lose your mind**
  to use your head.

**You lose your Mind
  to use your head.**

13

Turning On Is Sacred

Turning on is a complex, demanding, frightening, confusing

process.

Turning on requires diligent yoga.

Turning on requires a guide who can center you at the TV-stage-prop level and at the sensory, somatic, cellular, and molecular levels.

REMEMBER:

When you turn on

◉ You are not a naughty boy getting high for kicks.

◉ You are a spiritual voyager furthering the most ancient, noble quest of man.

◉ You shed the fake-prop TV studio and costume and join the holy dance of the visionaries.

◉ You leave LBJ, Geroge W and Bob Hope; you join Lao-tse, Christ, Blake.

You are a God.

Turn on
Tune In
Drop out

Never underestimate
the sacred meaning
of the turn-on.

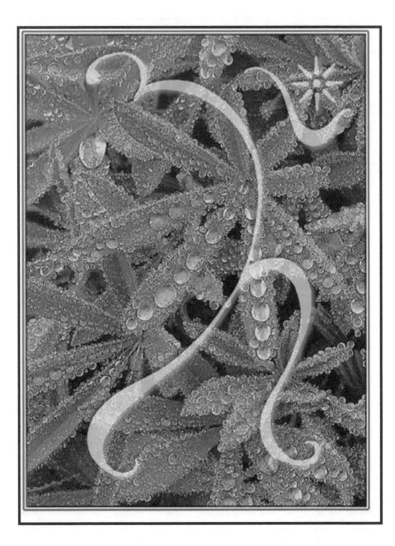

14
Use
A Sacrament

To turn on,

you need a sacrament.

A sacrament is a visible external
        thing which turns the key to
        the inner doors.

A sacrament must bring about
        bodily changes.

A sacrament flips you out of the
        TV-studio game and harnesses
        you to the 2 billion-year-old
        flow inside.

A sacrament that works is dangerous to the establishment that runs the fake-prop TV studio—and to that part of your mind which is hooked to the studio game.

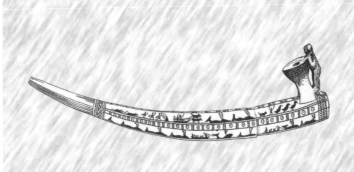

The true importance of LSD is the possibility of providing material aid to the mediation aimed at the mystical experience of a deeper, comprehensive reality. Such a use accords entirely with the essence and working character of LSD as a sacred drug.

—Albert Hofmann

Each TV-prop society produces exactly that body-changing sacrament which will flip out the mind of the society. Elements of social control does not readily understand the use of an active sacrament, such as that probably used by Socrates, Plato, Aristotle the Roman Emperor Marus Aurelius and other famous Greek and Romans in the Eleusinian mystery religious rites during the Classical ages.

In the 1960s and 70s, the sacrament is LSD. New sacraments are coming along.Sacraments wear out. They become part of the social TV-studio game.

15

How to Tune In

You cannot stay turned on all the time. You cannot stay anyplace all the time.

That's a law of evolution.

After the revelation it is
necessary to drop back in,
return to the fake-prop TV
studio and initiate small
changes which reflect the
glory and . . .

the meaning
of the turn-on.

You change the way you
move, the way you dress,
and you change your corner
of the TV-studio society.

You begin to look like a
happy saint. Your home
slowly becomes a shrine.
Slowly, gently, you start
seed transformations
around you.

Psychedelic art.
Psychedelic style.
Psychedelic music.
Psychedelic dance.

Suddenly you discover

YOU
have

dropped

out.

16
How to Drop Out

Drop out means exactly that:

Drop out.

Most of the activity of most Americans goes into robot performances on the TV-studio stage.

fake.

unnatural.

automatic.

DROP OUT means detach yourself from every TV drama which is not in the rhythm of the turn-on, tune-in, drop-out cycle.

Quit school.

Quit your job.

Don't vote. Avoid all politics.

Do not waste conscious thinking on TV- studio games.

Political choices

are meaningless.

To postpone the drop-out is to **cop out.**

Dismiss your fantasies of infiltrating the social stage-set game. Any control you have over television props is their control over you.

Dismiss the Judaic-Christian-Marxist-puritan-literary-existentialist suggestion that the drop-out is escape and that the conformist cop-out is reality.

Dropping out is the
hardest yoga of all.

Make your drop-out invisible.

No rebellion—please!

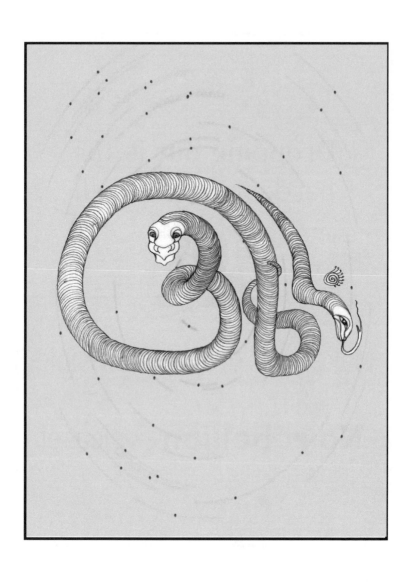

17

Form Your Own Cult

The drop-out, turn-on, tune-in rhythm is most naturally done in small groups of family members, lovers, and seed friends.

For psychedelic and legal reasons, you must form your own cult.

The directors of the TV studio do not want you to live a religious life.

They will apply every pressure—including prison—to keep you in their game.

Your own mind, which has been corrupted and neurologically damaged by years of education in fake-prop TV-studio games, will also keep you trapped in the game.

A group libertion cult is required.

You must form that
most ancient and sacred
of human structures—

The Clan.

Remember, you are basically a primate. You are designed by the 2-billion-year blueprint to live in a small band. You cannot accept the political or spiritual leadership of anyone you cannot touch, con-spire (breathe) with, worship with, get high with.

A clan or cult is a small group of human beings organized around a religious goal.

YOUR CLAN
MUST BE CENTERED
ON A SHRINE AND A TOTEM
SPIRITUAL ENERGY SOURCE.

To the clan you dedicate
your highest loyalty . . .

And to you the clan offers
its complete protection.

The clan must be centered on
religious goals.

Religion means being
tuned in to the natu-
ral rhythm.

Religion is the turn-on,
tune-on, drop-out
process.

You will

radiate energy!

Because you and your clan fellows are turned on,

You will **attract** attention-hostility from the TV establishment, enthusiastic interest from rootless TV actors who wish to join your clan.

Everyone basically
wants to turn on,
tune in, and
drop out.

Avoid conflict with
the establishment.

Avoid recruiting and
rapid growth.

Avoid commitments to
TV-studio power games

Preserve clan harmony.

Your clan must be limited to essential friends.

You must guard against the TV power tendency toward exp-a-n-s-i-o-n.

Your clan cannot become a mail-order, mass-numbers organization.

The structure of your clan must be cellular.

The center of
your religion must
be a private, holy
place.

The activities of
your religion must
be limited to the
turn-on, tune-in,
drop-out sequence.

Write your very own
Newest Testament,
remembering that ...

voluntary martyrdom is tacky
and

CRUCIFIXIONS,

like nuclear war,

can ruin your day.

No one can start
your religion for you.

You

must start

your

own religion.

You are
a God!

Act like one!

Discover and nurture
your divinity.

18
Search For Meaning

Those who use psychedelic chemicals—marijuana, peyote, LSD—must appraise their goals and games realistically.

You smoke pot? Why?

As part of your personality game?

As part of the American TV-studio
perspective?

To enhance your ego?

As part of your TV role as
hipster, sophisticate, rebel?

Because it is the in-thing to do
in your stage set?

Because it is a social-psychological
habit?

Good. Keep on.

The "pot game" is
a fascinating scenario to act out,
the entertaining game of
illicit kicks.

There is another way of viewing
psychedelic drugs, including pot:
from the perspective of history.

For thousands of years the greatest
artists, poets, philosophers, and lovers
have used consciousness-expanding
substances to turn on, tune in, drop out.

Why?

Because!

It is a step the search for
the meaning of life.

It offers tools to reach new
levels of awareness.

It helps to see beyond the
immediate social game.

It opens revelation—a light in
the darkness of the
long voyage.

Every great burst of activity has grown out of a psychedelic turn-on. The visionary then rushes back ...

to tune in ...

to pass on the message.

A new art form.

A new mode
   of expression.

He turns others on.

A cult is formed.

A new TV stage set is
   designed, one that is closer to the
   family-clan-tribal cell structure of our
   species.

**Do you wish to use
marijuana and LSD . . .**

To get beyond the TV scenario?

To enhance creativity?

As catalysts to deepen wisdom?

If so, you will be helped by
making explicit the religious
nature of your psychedelic
activities ...

◆ to give meaning to your own
script, to clarify your
relationships with others,
and

◆ to cope with the legal setup.

You will do well
to start your
own religion.

19

How to Start
Your Own Religion

First, decide with whom you
will make the voyage of
discovery.

If you have a **family,** certainly you
will include them.

If you have **close friends**, you
will certainly want to include them.

With Whom Do I League
for Spiritual Discovery?

List all of the people who are candidates for
sharing your adventure of spiritual discovery.
Anwering this question is a fascinating exercise.

◆

◆

◆

◆

◆

◆

◆

◆

Next, gather your spiritual companions in a group, sit down and write
down the plan for your spiritual trip.

Write down and define each of the following:

◆ Goals:

◆ Roles:

◆ Rituals:

◆ Rules:

◆ Vocabulary:

◆ Values:

◆ Space-time locales:

◆ Mythic context:

Defining the structural components of your religion is an interesting exercise.

You will learn a lot about yourself and your companions.

You will see where you are and where you are not.

How will your clan handle the following touchy issues?

Be explicit. Write it down.

◆ Authority:

◆ Responsibility:

◆ Sexual Relations:

◆ Money & Bills:

◆ Conflict:

◆ Communication:

You are forming not only your own religion but your own natural political unit. Did you really believe that church was only where you went for an hour on Sunday morning?

The basic political unit is exactly the same as the basic spiritual grouping:

The Clan.

Make your clan unique.

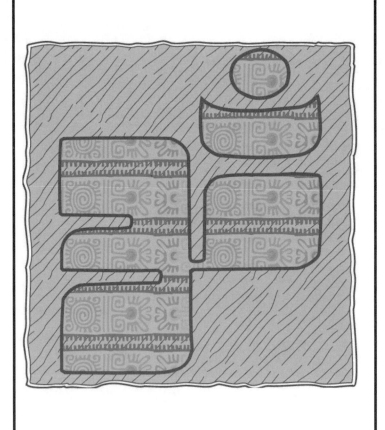

20
Make Your Religion Unique

The aim of clan living is to subordinate the ego game to the family game—

the clan game.

**Do not slavishly copy the roles
and language of other groups.**

The beauty of cellular life
is that each unit is both so
incredibly complexly similar and also so unique.

The more you understand
the infinite complexity of life,
the more you treasure both
the similarities and the
differences.

But you have to be
turned on to see it.

At the level of the studio prop game, both the similarities and the differences are trivial.

In defining the goal of *your* religion:

You need not use conventional religious language.

You don't have to make your spiritual journey *sound* "religious."

Don't be **intimidated** by Caesar's Hollywood fake versions of religiosity.

Religion cannot be pompous and
high flown.

Religion is *consciousness exp a n s i o n,*

centered in
the body

and

defined exactly
the way it
sounds best to

you.

If life has a meaning for you
beyond the TV studio game,

YOU are religious!

Spell it out.

Write out your plan for the trip:

- ✦ God *or* Evolution,

- ✦ Acid *or* Sacrament,

- ✦ Guide *or* Guru,

- ✦ Purgatorial redemption
  or Bad trip,

- ✦ Mystic revelation
  or Good high.

Say it naturally.

21

Develop Your Own Rituals

Develop your own rituals and costumes—

robes or gray flannel suits,

amulets or tattoos.

You will eventually find
yourself engaged in a series
of sacred moments that feel
right to you.

Step-by-step
all your
actions will
take on a
sacramental
meaning.

Inevitably you will create a ritual
sequence for each sense organ and
for each of the basic energy
exchanges:

> eating,
>
> bathing,
>
> mating, etc.

You must be
explicit about
the space-time
arrangement for
your God Game.

Make your home
a spiritual center.

Place a
shrine in
each room.

Regular rhythms of worship emerge:

Daily meditation (turn-on) sessions
with or without sacrament.

Once a week or once a month
devote a whole day to turning on.

Time your worship
to the rhythm
of the seasons,
to the planetary calendar

The CHURCH OF WOW

Primal Energetics & AXIS MUNDI World Groove Trance Chant invite you to join us for an EQUINOX CELEBRATION of AMRITA & THE TEMPLE WITHIN - Fluid Embodiment of the Emotional Soul.

Celebrate the Alchemical Moment of the Year when the Primal Energies of Light and Dark, Without and Within, are in Perfect Balance. This truly special gathering will unite the CHURCH OF WOW Primal Energetics, and the Voyager Tarot in creative collaboration with AXIS MUNDI Sacred Sonic Ritualists and the extended Spirit Tribe Collective.

We will launch off on a shamanic journey exploring Inherent Emotional Intelligence, authentic Ecstatic Energy, and Embodied Yearning. This quantum terrain arises from the Temple Within—triggered by Breath, Sound, Movement, & the sweet drip of "Immortal Time Essence" AMRITA within the fructifying CAVES of our own bodies.

PRIMAL ENERGETICS Participatory Demo with **WOWZA!** Primal Energetics reclaims what has been lost—the natural genius of free-spirited emotive authenticity and unstudied grace of movement.

A new, quantum body language is introduced which supports the fluid embodiment of eight emotional energies with breath, sound, and movement. With an inherent emotional intelligence, we posses a driving intent to express the beauty and power of our originality.

TRANCE DANCE to AXIS MUNDI Sonic Shamanic Trance Chant. Experience the Ecstasy of the Vedic Cave Rituals of ancient India!

AXIS MUNDI's powerful devotional Chant revives the timeless ritual of Shakti-Shiva's Dance—the Spontaneously Arising Ecstatic Agony of Endless Bliss born at the dawn of Consciousness.

Journey through the mystical dimensions of Coherent Emotion & Primal Yearning in Trance Dancing & Dynamic Whole Body Meditation.

Make Your Church Unique

22
Money & Work

Money is a completely irrational focus for most Westerners.

Spell out on paper explicit plans for handling financial interactions.

When your clan members detach themselves emotionally from money, you will discover how easy it is to survive economically.

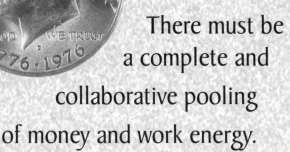

There must be
a complete and
collaborative pooling
of money and work energy.

Any selfish holding back of

dollars or muscular energy

will weaken **the clan**.

Each clan
will develop
its own
productivity.

Each clan, as it drops
out of the American
game, must appraise
its resources and
figure out how to
barter with other
groups

The Dog Commune

While using LSD in the late 1960's, commune founders received visions that God existed on Earth incarnate in dogs, and that all of humanity's ills can be traced to the mistreatment of man's best friend—dogs! Commune members herded dogs and raided animal shelters to liberate their deities. They tried to raise public consciousness about animal exploitation in research labs.

23
Sexuality

ex is sacred.

But sexuality is the downfall of most religious cults.

Your mode of sexual union
is the key to your religion.

You cannot escape this.

The way you ball (or avoid balling) is your central sacramental activity.

Clarity and honesty are necessary.

Each man is made to mate with one woman.

Heterosexual
monogamous
fidelity is the

only natural way
of sexual union.

Karmic
accidental
differences
exist in people's
sexual makeup.

This is the Kali Yoga.

We live in the final
stages of a sick
society, sexual
variations are
inevitable.

**The sexual
proclivity of the
clan must be
explicit and
inflexible.**

Do not attempt to establish clan
relationships with persons of a
different sexual persuasion.

People of like sexual
temperament must
form their own
spiritual cults.

There is no value judgment here.

Homosexuality is not an illness.

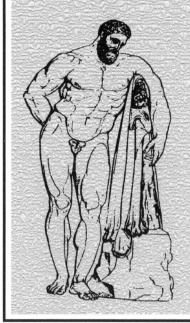

It is a religious
way of life.

Homosexuals should accept their
state as a religious path.

Homosexuals cannot join heterosexual clans.

Homosexuals should
treasure and glorify
their own sexual yoga.

Heterosexual clans can support, help, learn from, teach homosexual clans, but the difference must be preserved with mutual respect. Their right to pursue their sacred bodily yoga is guaranteed to them.

Some spiritual people
are not compatible with the
monogamous union and prefer
a freer sexual regime:

The Group Marriage.

Many tribes and clans
throughout the planet
have flourished in
complete and holy
promiscuity.

But be explicit.

Painful confusions occur if sexual orientations and sexual taboos—cellular and physical, not psychological or cultural— are disregarded in forming clans.

Select clan members who share or complement:

your style,

your way of tuning in,

your temperament,

your sexual orientation.

24

Connect To Mythic Orgins

You will do well to have an explicit connection to a mythic figure.

Know your mythic origins.

Myths humanize
the recurrent themes
of evolution.

Facts and news are
reports from the
current TV drama.

They have no relevance
to your 2-billionyear-old
divinity.

Myth is the report
from the cellular
memory bank.

Select a Guiding Myth:

Select a myth to guide you when
you drop out of the narrow
confines of the fake-prop
studio set.

Select a myth as a reminder that
you are part of an ancient and
holy process.

Select a myth that answers
the death-rebirth riddle.

a tv drama hero cannot help you.

Caesar, Napoleon, Kennedy
are no help to your cellular
orientation.

Christ. Lao-tse, Hermes
Trismegistus, Socrates
are recurrent turn-on
figures

25

Go to the Land

Y ou will find it absolutely
necessary to leave the city.

Urban living is spiritual suicidal.

The cities of America
are about to crumble as
did Rome and Babylon.
Go to the land.
Go to the sea.

© Providence Lithograph Co.

Thousands of spiritual seekers come to urban districts where they meet in meditation enters and psychedelic assemble places.

They form their clans.

They migrate from the city.

26
Do It Yourself

U nless you form your own new religion and devote an increasing amount of your energies to it, no matter how exciting your personality TV role—

You are a robot!

Your new religion
can be formed
only by you.

Do not wait for a messiah.

Do it yourself!

The goals, roles, rules, rituals, values, language, space-tie locale, and mythic context of your religion must be put on paper for two reasons.

One, to make the journey clear and explicit for yourself and your clan members, and

Two, to deal with Caesar.

the RELationship between Caesar and the God Seeker has always been uneasy.

But the boundaries of the tension can be defined precisely, and if you are clear in your mind, there can be no confusion.

You can move with exactness and confidence.

Everything that exists outside your body and your shrine belongs to Caesar.

Caesar has constructed
the fake-prop studio
for his king-of-the-mountain
game, and he can have it.

Highways, property, status,
power, money, weapons,
all things, all external
man-made objects
belong to him.

The spiritual life is
completely detached
from these props.

Obey Caesar's TV studio rules
when you are in his studios.

Avoid any participation
in his dramas.

**Operate below the radar
of the authorities.**

27
The Kingdom Of Heaven

Your body is the kingdom of heaven, and your home is the shrine in which the kingdom of heaven is to be found.

What you do inside *your* body ...

What energies you let contact
your sense organs, and ...

What you put into *your* body ...

Is your
business!

All you need do to protect
the divinity of your body
and the sanctity of your
shrine is to
be explicit—
and to
worship
with dignity
and courage.

Remember:

You are

a God!

Write down an eightfold definition of your religion— define your goals, roles, rules, rituals, values, languages, myths, space-time locales .

By doing so,
you have formed
your religion.

28
Make Your Home A Shrine

Your right to turn on in your home is sacred.

MAKE YOUR HOME
A SHRINE BY WRITING
IT INTO THE CHARTER
OF YOUR RELIGION.

Specify visible objects of worship
which will be found in your shrine—
a statue of Buddha, a picture of
Christ, a rock, a wooden carving.

The charter does not permit you to turn on just anywhere.

In writing your charter,

specify where you will take the sacrament and with whom.

Respect the possessive claims of Caesar to his fake-front stage sets.

If you take a psychedelic sacrament, leave your house and commit a disorder on Caesar's streets; *then* let him arrest you for an overt crime.

It is not advised that a church have multiple Euchasists. When the courts have considered religious defenses of illicit drug use, they have only listened to arguments involving one sacrament. The rational is that an entheogenic sacrament might be valid only if it is essential and indispensable in the practice of the faith. When a church has multiple sacraments the implication is that no one sacrament is essential.

You choose, but be explicit.

29

Retain An Attorney

Don't be surprised at the idea of having a lawyer to handle your sacramental affairs. For a small amount of money you can have ongoing legal protection for your religion.

Incorporate your religion.
Then file the application forms
and a description of methods of
worship in the
attorney's office.

In case of any misunderstanding with Caesar's cops, you will be effectively prepared.

Well, according to The Bill of Rights.

Many Americans were disappointed that the
Constitution did not contain a bill of rights
that would explicitly enumerate the rights of
American citizens and enable courts and
public opinion to protect these rights from
an oppressive government. Supporters of a
bill of rights permitted the Constitution to be
adopted with the understanding that the first
Congress under the new government would
attempt to add a bill of rights.

James Madison took the lead in steering such a bill through the First Federal Congress, which convened in the spring of 1789. The Virginia Ratifying Convention and Madison's constituents, among whom were large numbers of Baptists who wanted freedom of religion secured, expected him to push for a bill of rights. On September 28, 1789, both houses of Congress voted to send twelve amendments to the states. In December 1791, those ratified by the requisite three fourths of the states became the first ten amendments to the Constitution. Religion was addressed in the First Amendment in the following familiar words: *"Congress shall make no law respecting an establishment of religion, or prohibiting the free exercise thereof."* In notes for his June 8, 1789, speech introducing the Bill of Rights, Madison indicated his opposition to a "national" religion. Most Americans agreed that the federal government must not pick out one religion and give it exclusive financial and legal support.

30

Get A Declaratory Judgement

There is a another legal step which some brave psychedelic religionists will want to take— the licensing for the importation and distribution of illegal sacraments, such as marijuana and LSD.

The legal procedure involved in obtaining permission to use drugs is called a *declaratory judgment.*

This procedure can result in a court declaration that an individual or a group may, with the sanction of law, use drugs freely for religious purposes.

In requesting a declaratory judgment to import and distribute illegal sacraments—

and remember here that alcohol, nicotine, and automobiles are also illegal, except to licensed operators—

You are asking nothing more than was permitted to Catholic priests and Jewish rabbis during alcohol prohibition.

These religionists were allowed to import and distribute an illegal drug—booze—for distribution only by priests and only in designated shrines.

The quarter of a million members of the Native American Church are similarly licensed to use peyote, a plant much more powerful than marijuana.

The filing for a declaratory judgment requires more commitment and energy—*and it is risky!* Thus this becomes the third test of your religious stamina.

In a 1991 case related to peyote (*Lophophora williamsii*) U.S. District Chief Judge Juan Burciago stated:

> *"The government's war on drugs has become a Wildfire . . . the war targets one of the most deeply held fundamental rights— the First Amendment right to freely exercise one's religion."*

31

Reality Check

I smile when I look back on my enthusiasm—

and naivete.

I used to think that we could look to the Constitution to protect our Right to religious freedom, including the use of mind-altering sacraments.

We now know that churches that legally incorporate and that openly use entheogenic sacraments are not likely to be permitted by authorities to exercise their religious freedoms.

these
RENEGRADE
churches are
making a **noble**
stand for **our**
constitutional
Rights.

In the face of Caesar's persecution, there are still many underground churches.

Their rituals and prayers are usually rooted in psychedelic trip therapy, shamanism and Eastern Mysticism. There are numerous ayahuasca circles, especially in California. These underground churches operate below the radar of the authorities.

Turn on

Tune in

Drop out

Below the radar . . . .